Brain Bot: Keep Your Brain Young with ChatGPT

Use AI to Keep Your Mind Sharp by Sugar Gay Isber McMillan

ISBN: 978-1-967973-79-8

This book is for educational purposes only. It is not a medical book and does not diagnose, treat, or prevent any condition. The information in this book is not a substitute for advice from a qualified medical or mental health professional. All exercises are optional. Readers should use their own judgment and consult a professional if needed.

Printed in the United States of America
The WOW Book Co.

Large Font Edition

For more books in this series visit:
The WOW Book Co.

BRAIN
Bot
Keep Your Brain Young with ChatGPT
Use AI to Keep Your Mind Sharp
Sugar Gay Isber McMillan

Disclaimer

This book is not a medical guide or a diagnostic tool. It does not provide medical advice or claim to treat any condition.

This book teaches you how to use ChatGPT as a thinking companion to keep your mind active.

If you have concerns about memory, cognition, mood, or any health issue, speak with a licensed medical professional.

ChatGPT can make mistakes.

Always check important information.

Companion Book Available

Brain Bot: 400 Plus Puzzles and Daily Brain Challenges

If you enjoy the exercises in this book, explore the full companion volume filled with more than four hundred puzzles, games, pattern drills, riddles, logic warm-ups and memory boosters designed to keep your brain young.

This companion book includes:

- Visual pattern puzzles
- Short logic sequences
- Memory and recall drills
- Wordplay challenges
- Number patterns
- Five-minute focus builders
- Daily warm-ups for mental clarity

It pairs perfectly with *Brain Bot: Keep Your Brain Young with ChatGPT* and gives you a full year of brain-strengthening activities.

Ask for:

Brain Bot: 400 Plus Puzzles and Daily Brain Challenges
Published by The WOW Book Co.

Search Sugar Gay Isber McMillan Books on Amazon

Table of Contents

Introduction

You can keep your brain young. You can stay sharp, curious, and confident at any age. The research is clear. People who stay engaged with technology and learning enjoy better memory, stronger problem-solving, and lower cognitive decline. Your brain thrives when you give it something new to work with.

That is exactly what this book will do for you.

You do not need to be "good with computers" to use ChatGPT. You only need curiosity and a few minutes a day. ChatGPT is patient, fast, and ready whenever you are. It never gets tired. It never judges. And it works at your pace.

You also do not have to type. This is important because many people feel nervous when they see a keyboard. You can simply press the microphone and speak. ChatGPT listens in real time and turns your voice into text on the screen.

You do not need to correct your words. You do not need perfect grammar. You do not even have to speak quickly. Just talk like you talk to a friend. The microphone stays open as long as you want, so you can think, pause or gather your thoughts without rushing.

This makes ChatGPT easy for anyone, regardless of age, to use. Your job is only to talk. ChatGPT does the rest.

This book will show you how to:

- Keep your mind active
- Practice memory, attention, and quick thinking
- Learn new things every day

• Have more fun and stay mentally engaged
• Use ChatGPT in simple, practical, brain-friendly ways

You will learn how to do all of this in short daily sessions. Ten minutes a day can change everything.

Your Brain Bot is here. Let's get started.

A Note About Computer ChatGPT and Phone ChatGPT

Your computer version of ChatGPT and your phone version of ChatGPT look a little different and do not always match each other. This is normal. Each one saves your chats separately. This means a conversation you start on your computer may not appear on your phone, and a chat you start on your phone may not show up on your computer.

Nothing is wrong when this happens. The two versions are built differently because many people use only one device. You can use either one and they will both work well.

Here is the best way to think about it:

• Your computer ChatGPT is good for long conversations, reading, and typing
• Your phone ChatGPT is good for voice dictation, quick questions, and simple tasks on the go

You can use both whenever you want. Just remember that each device saves its own history. If you want to keep something important, copy and paste it into a document or email so you always have a record of it.

This keeps everything simple and stress-free.

Note: This book is not a medical guide. It does not diagnose, treat or prevent any condition. It teaches you how to use ChatGPT as a thinking partner for mental stimulation, creativity and daily organization. Always consult a licensed professional for medical or cognitive concerns.

Chapter 1

How to Use ChatGPT the Easy Way

Welcome. This is your Brain Bot talking to you. You are about to begin something that will keep your mind young, curious, and strong. ChatGPT makes learning easy. It makes thinking easier. It keeps your brain active with almost no effort on your part.

You do not need to be good with computers. You do not need to type fast. You do not need to know any special words. You only need to take simple steps in this Chapter.

Many people skip the introduction, so we are starting fresh right here. This Chapter will show you how to open ChatGPT, how to talk to it, and how to get helpful answers, even if this is your first time. Everything you learn from now on will be easy, friendly, and designed to help your brain stay sharp.

By the end of this Chapter, you will be able to speak to ChatGPT, ask questions, and use your Brain Bot as a daily partner.

---

1. You Do Not Need to Type

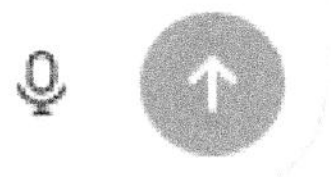

Use the Microphone and Talk Naturally**

Most people think they have to type every message. You do not. Talking is easier. Talking is faster. Talking feels natural and keeps your brain calm.

Here is how dictation works on a phone or tablet:

1. Tap the microphone
2. Talk in your normal voice
3. Pause when you want to think
4. Keep going when you are ready
5. Tap the arrow to send your message

You do not need to fix anything. You do not need perfect grammar. You do not need to worry if a word shows up wrong. ChatGPT understands what you meant.

You can leave the microphone open while you think. You do not need to tap it on and off between every sentence. Speak slow or fast, whatever feels natural. Think of it as talking to a friend sitting beside you.

Talking uses more parts of the brain than typing. This is one of the reasons Brain Bot training works so well.

---

2. How to Open ChatGPT on a Computer

Many beginners feel comfortable starting here.

1. Open your web browser
2. Go to ChatGPT.com

3. Log in or create a free account
4. Click "New Chat"
5. You will see a blank box at the bottom of the screen

Your computer version uses your keyboard only. If you want to speak instead of type, use your computer's built-in voice-to-text tool. Nothing you do can break anything.

---

3. How to Open ChatGPT on a Phone or Tablet

The phone and tablet versions have the easiest layout for beginners.

1. Open the ChatGPT app
2. Tap "New Chat"
3. Tap the microphone
4. Begin talking
5. Tap the arrow to send your message

You do not have to type a single word.

---

4. Your Computer ChatGPT and Your Phone ChatGPT Are Different

These two versions do not sync your conversations. This surprises many people.

Chats you start on your computer may not appear on your phone. Chats you start on your phone may not appear on your computer. Each device has its own history.

Nothing is wrong when this happens.

Think of them as two separate notebooks that both work well.

If you want to save something important, copy and paste it into a document or send it to yourself in an email.

---

5. Talk to ChatGPT Like a Partner

ChatGPT responds to your tone. You can talk to it like a person.

Say things like:

- "Brain Bot, help me plan my morning."
- "Brain Bot, explain this slowly."
- "Brain Bot, help me stay calm and focused."
- "Brain Bot, guide me through a simple task."

This is natural. You can talk out loud, think out loud, ask for help, or tell it what is going on in your day. ChatGPT is patient and never rushes you.

---

6. How ChatGPT Learns You

Building the Brain of Your Bot**

Your Brain Bot becomes better the more you use it.

The first time you open ChatGPT, it does not know you yet. It does not know what you like, how you talk, or what you need. As you speak, ChatGPT listens to the patterns in your questions and your style. It learns your preferences. It learns how you think. It learns what you need help with.

The more you talk to it, the more it becomes your partner.

This is how you strengthen the brain of the bot:

- Tell it about your interests
- Share your routines
- Tell it your goals
- Tell it what you want help with
- Ask it to adjust to your voice or style
- Remind it of what matters to you

Your Brain Bot will grow with you. Every conversation shapes it.

This is why daily use keeps everything easy.

---

7. What the Little Icons Mean

You will see small icons around your chat window. Here is what they do:

Copy icon
Makes a copy of ChatGPT's answer so you can paste it elsewhere.

Thumbs up
Tells ChatGPT that the answer was helpful.

Thumbs down

Tells ChatGPT the answer missed what you needed.

Refresh arrow

Gives you a new version of the answer.

Upload icon

Lets you attach a picture or file. ChatGPT can read images and PDFs.

Three dots

Shows extra options, depending on your device.

You do not need to use any of these to begin. They are there for when you feel comfortable exploring.

---

8. How to Ask Your First Question

Keep your first message simple.

Try:

- "Brain Bot, help me get started."
- "Brain Bot, teach me something in one minute."
- "Brain Bot, ask me a fun question."

Or choose a topic:

- "Tell me something interesting about birds."
- "Give me a short memory exercise."
- "Help me focus for five minutes."

Your Brain Bot will respond right away.

---

9. A Simple First Exercise

Say:

"Brain Bot, give me a gentle warm up that is easy for beginners."

You may get a short puzzle, a small question, or a tiny challenge. This is enough to activate your brain for the day.

---

10. Your First Daily Routine

Try this every morning:

"Brain Bot, help me start my day. Ask me what matters most today and help me focus."

This builds clarity and confidence.

---

11. When You Feel Confused

Remember:

- You cannot break anything
- You cannot get in trouble
- You will never be judged
- There are no wrong questions
- You can repeat steps anytime

You are learning a new skill in a safe place.

---

12. What Comes Next

When you finish this Chapter, you will know how to:

- Open ChatGPT
- Use your voice instead of typing
- Understand the basic buttons
- Use ChatGPT on both computer and phone
- Ask your first questions
- Begin easy brain training
- Build your Brain Bot's memory of you over time

This foundation carries you through the rest of the book. Each new Chapter adds another layer of strength, clarity, and mental energy.

---

13. How to Keep Your Chats Organized

Projects and Chat Names**

When you use ChatGPT every day, your chats can fill up quickly. Most people do not know that you can organize everything so it stays neat and easy to find later. You do this with **Projects** and by **renaming individual chats**.

Here is the difference:

What a Chat Is

A chat is one conversation.
It might be a brain exercise, a question, a recipe, or a short task.
Chats can get long and messy if you keep everything in one place.

You can rename any chat so it is easy to recognize later.
Tap the chat title at the top and type a simple name.
Examples:

- Brain Bot Warmups
- Memory Exercises
- Daily Planning Chat

This keeps everything clear.

What a Project Is

A Project is a container that holds many chats, files, and notes in one place.
Think of it like a folder for bigger subjects.

If you are working through this book, you can make a Project called **Brain Bot** and store everything inside it:

- Your warm-up chats
- Your puzzles
- Your daily routines
- Your questions
- Your progress notes
- Any PDFs or screenshots you upload

This keeps all your brain training in one place.
Nothing gets lost. Nothing gets buried in old conversations.

Why This Helps New Users

If you start organizing from the very beginning, you will always know where things are. It keeps your Brain Bot work clean, simple, and easy to return to whenever you want.

How to Create Your First Project

On a computer:

1. Click "Projects"
2. Click "New Project"
3. Name it something simple, like "Brain Bot"
4. Move your chats into it or start new ones inside the project

On a phone, the layout may look different, but the steps are the same.

Start this now. It will make everything easier as you go through the book.

---

14. When a Chat Gets Full or Starts Acting Strange

Every long chat gets heavy over time. When this happens, ChatGPT can slow down, forget instructions, or answer in a way that feels off. This is normal. It is not your fault.

Here are the signs that a chat is getting "tired":

- Answers start repeating
- It takes longer to respond
- The wheel spins for too long
- It forgets details you already explained
- It ignores your writing preferences
- The screen freezes or your microphone stops working
- The tone feels different than before

This means the chat is full and needs a rest.

What to Do

Start a new chat.

Say:
"Brain Bot, we are starting fresh. Here is what I want you to remember."

Then restate your preferences in two or three short lines. That is all you need.

You can also place the old chat inside your Brain Bot project so you can return to anything important.

---

15. When You Should Refresh vs When You Should Restart

Refreshing is good when:

- You want the answer rewritten
- You want a clearer version
- You want a different tone
- You want new examples

Restarting is good when:

- The answers feel confused
- The bot forgets your style
- The chat is very long
- The page starts glitching
- The dictation stops working

This helps beginners know what to do instead of feeling frustrated.

---

16. How to Tell ChatGPT What You Want Every Time

Your Brain Bot works best when you remind it of your preferences at the start of a new chat. You can paste this sentence anytime:

"Brain Bot, keep your writing simple, friendly, and easy to understand. No emojis, no Oxford comma, and guide me one step at a time."

This resets everything and keeps your experience smooth.

---

17. How to Get a Better Answer if You Do Not Like the First One

Many people do not know they can ask for changes.

Try:

- "Make this shorter"
- "Make it slower and simpler"
- "Give me examples"
- "Try again in a different way"
- "Explain this like you are teaching a beginner"
- "Give me a version that feels calm"

This teaches readers how to "drive" ChatGPT instead of accepting whatever appears.

---

18. How to Keep Your Brain Bot Chat Clean and Simple

Two habits will help:

1. **Start a new chat for each new topic**
2. **Name the chat so you can find it later**

Examples:

• Brain Bot Memory Day
• Brain Bot Morning Plan
• Brain Bot Puzzle Session
• Brain Bot Calm Thinking

This keeps everything clear and your bot stays sharp.

---

19. A Simple Way to Reset Your Bot's Mind

If something feels off, say:

"Brain Bot, take a deep breath with me and reset. Let's start again. Here is what I need."

This works every time.

At the end of each chapter, there will be a small puzzle as an example. On the last page is the puzzle key so you can easily flip to the back of the book to check your answers. There are no tests; this is just an activity for you to learn from.

Answers to all the puzzles are listed on the final page, Puzzle Key.

Puzzle 1: Word Ladder

Change **COLD** to **WARM** by switching one letter at a time.
Each step must form a real word.

Companion note:
To make more puzzles like this, ask ChatGPT to create new word ladders or look for the Brain Bot companion puzzle book.

Your Brain Bot is ready.
Let's continue.

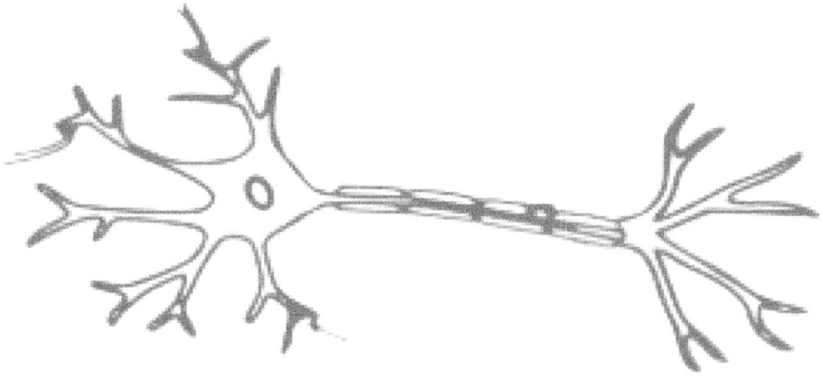

Chapter 2

Ask Your Bot to Help You Keep Your Brain Young

A simple guide for beginners who want a sharper mind

Keeping your brain young is not about doing hard things. It is about doing the right things every day. ChatGPT can guide you, coach you, and provide custom brainwork tailored to your age, energy, and interests. You do not have to guess what to do. You ask. Your bot delivers. That is the magic.

This Chapter shows you how to start.

---

1. Start With One Simple Goal

Before you ever type a prompt, decide what you want your brain to feel like.

Do you want:

- Better focus
- A stronger memory
- Clearer thinking
- Faster recall
- More confidence when you speak
- A steady mood
- A better sense of direction
- Support for your creativity

Pick one. ChatGPT can build a plan around it.

Try this starter prompt:

Prompt:
"My goal is to keep my brain young. I want to improve my _____. Give me a simple daily plan that takes ten minutes."

Your bot will create a list you can follow today.

---

2. Ask for Brain Workouts That Match Your Energy

Some days you want something easy. Some days you want a challenge. With ChatGPT, you never have to use an app you do not like or a puzzle that is too hard.

You can ask for the exact level you want.

Prompt:
"Give me an easy ten-minute brain warm-up for today. Make it fun."

Prompt:
"Give me a harder twenty-minute challenge that works my memory and attention."

ChatGPT will adjust for your age, your comfort level, and your learning style.

---

3. Use ChatGPT to Strengthen All Six Major Brain Skills

Most brain training companies focus on only one thing. ChatGPT can train all six.

1. Long-term memory
2. Short-term memory

3. Attention to detail
4. Executive function
5. Processing speed
6. Verbal fluency

Here is how to ask:

Prompt:
"Create a short exercise that trains long-term memory. Make it something I can do right now."
Prompt:
"Give me a simple game that strengthens processing speed."

This is the most flexible brain coach you will ever meet.

---

4. Ask for Puzzles You Can Do at Any Age

Crosswords. Word ladders. Memory chains. Category games. Observation drills. Pattern-spotting. Story recall. Most people do only one type. ChatGPT can rotate them for you so you never get bored.

Some examples:

Prompt:
"Give me a five-question trivia quiz about the 1970s."
Prompt:
"Give me a word ladder that starts with CAT and ends with MOON."
Prompt:
"Give me a visual observation challenge I can do without pictures."

Prompt:
"Give me a memory chain with ten items. Test me after."

These are simple to ask and fun to do.

---

5. Ask for Gentle Coaching When You Get Stuck

Many adults stop doing puzzles because they get frustrated. ChatGPT removes the frustration and keeps the brain benefits.

Try this:

Prompt:
"I am stuck. Give me a hint that does not give away the answer."

or

Prompt:
"Explain this puzzle in a friendlier way."

A little support goes a long way.

---

6. Let ChatGPT Track Your Growth

You do not need an app or a notebook. Your bot can keep a record for you.

Prompt:
"Create a simple weekly brain-health log. Ask me three questions every day and save my answers so you can measure my progress."

This creates accountability and momentum. Even five minutes a day helps.

---

7. Ask for Activities That Fit Your Real Life

Strong brain health comes from variety.

You can ask for:

- One puzzle
- One memory challenge
- One creativity spark
- One conversation topic
- One observation exercise
- One mini logic problem

Here is how:

Prompt:
"Give me a daily brain routine with five small tasks I can finish in fifteen minutes."

This is the simplest way to build a younger brain at any age.

---

8. Turn Boring Moments into Brain Moments

Waiting in line. Sitting in a doctor's office. Waiting for a friend. You can turn any moment into brain-training time by asking:

Prompt:
"Give me a fast two-minute mental game I can do right now."

This keeps your mind active without stress.

---

9. Let ChatGPT Personalize Everything to You

Reading glasses. Hearing issues. Trouble with tiny fonts. Difficulty typing fast. No problem.

You can say:

Prompt:
"Make everything larger and easier to read."
Prompt:
"Give me puzzles that do not require fast typing."
Prompt:
"I need slower instructions."

Your bot meets you where you are.

---

10. Celebrate the Small Wins

ChatGPT can help you see the progress you miss.

Prompt:
"Tell me what I did well this week based on my routine."

Feeling progress is key to staying motivated.

Puzzle 2: Memory Sequence

Read these numbers once. Then look away and write them from memory:
4 – 17 – 3 – 12 – 29 – 8 – 15

Companion note:
Use ChatGPT to generate new number recall drills or explore the companion puzzle book.

Chapter 3

Daily Brain Workouts with ChatGPT**

Your brain is designed to grow, adapt, and strengthen at any age. You simply need the right inputs. In this Chapter, you will learn how to turn ChatGPT into your personal brain trainer. Every activity is simple and each one builds real cognitive strength.

Think of this as your ten-minute routine. Short practices. Big impact. You will begin forming a habit that keeps your mind sharp and flexible. You can return to these exercises anytime.

1. Warm Up Your Mind With Quick Prompts

Start every session with a gentle stretch for your thinking. These take less than two minutes and get your brain ready for deeper work.

Try one of these warm-ups:

• "Give me one interesting fact from history. Make me guess before telling me the answer."
• "Give me a simple logic puzzle to warm up my mind."
• "Give me one new vocabulary word. Ask me to use it in a sentence."

These are small. They signal to your brain that learning time has begun. The goal is not perfection. The goal is activation.

2. Improve Your Memory Using Guided Recall

Your memory sharpens when you practice retrieving information. ChatGPT can walk you through simple recall sessions that feel like games.

Ask:

- "Give me five items to memorize. Test me after one minute."
- "Tell me a short story. Ask me to recall key details."
- "Give me three facts about the world. Quiz me later in the session."

This teaches your brain to hold and pull information forward. Retrieval is one of the strongest ways to keep your mind young.

3. Strengthen Your Attention and Focus

A wandering mind is normal. A trained mind is powerful. ChatGPT can help you tighten your focus in short bursts.

Try:

- "Give me a paragraph with one mistake. Help me find it."
- "Give me a pattern of letters. Ask me to spot the odd one out."
- "Challenge me with a two-minute concentration puzzle."

These exercises improve your ability to notice details and stay present. That skill supports every area of life.

4. Build Flexibility With Creative Challenges

Flexibility is your ability to shift thinking when the world shifts around you. It is one of the first skills to decline when the brain is not challenged. The good news is that it is also one of the easiest to rebuild.

Ask:

- "Give me one object. Ask me to list ten unexpected uses for it."
- "Give me a boring sentence. Ask me to rewrite it in three different styles."

• "Give me a problem. Ask me to brainstorm solutions from three viewpoints."

Creative flexibility keeps your thinking light. It helps you adapt faster. It helps you stay confident.

5. Speed Up Your Processing With Timed Drills

A quick mind often comes from light daily speed work. ChatGPT can run the drills for you and time each round.

Try:

• "Give me five math problems I can solve in ten seconds each."
• "Give me a category. Ask me to list as many items as possible in one minute."
• "Give me rapid-fire questions. Start with easy ones and increase the pace."

This improves processing speed. Think of it as interval training for your brain.

6. Grow New Neural Pathways Through Novelty

Novelty wakes up the brain. When you learn something new, your brain fires in fresh patterns. Over time, those patterns become strong pathways.

Ask:

• "Teach me one small thing I did not know."
• "Take me on a five-minute tour of a topic I have never explored."
• "Show me how to see something familiar in a new way."

Small doses of novelty produce significant long-term gains in cognitive health.

7. Use ChatGPT to Build a Ten Minute Daily Routine

Here is a sample routine you can copy:

Minute 1: Warm up with a fact or quick puzzle
Minutes 2 to 3: Memory game
Minutes 4 to 5: Attention drill
Minutes 6 to 7: Creative flexibility challenge
Minutes 8 to 9: Speed drill
Minute 10: Novel idea of the day

You can keep this routine or ask ChatGPT to create a new one every morning. The structure works because it blends memory, attention, creativity, speed, and novelty in a short window of time.

8. Why These Exercises Work

These are not random games. They target major cognitive systems that matter at every stage of life.

- Memory
- Attention
- Processing speed
- Problem solving
- Language
- Flexibility

You can strengthen these areas. Science shows they respond very well to consistent daily stimulation. Even ten minutes is enough to make a measurable difference.

9. How to Track Your Progress

Progress is simple to track. You do not need a chart. You only need to notice the small changes that appear over time.

Ask yourself:

- Am I thinking faster?
- Am I recalling things more easily?
- Do I feel more mentally awake?
- Am I less frustrated when learning something new?
- Does my mind feel steadier and confident?

These changes are signs of cognitive growth. They are the markers of a young and active brain.

10. Your Brain Is Not Fixed

You can improve at any age. You can get sharper. You can grow new pathways. You can feel mentally strong. You can build confidence through small, daily steps.

ChatGPT is the easiest way to begin. It is patient. It adapts to your pace. It never judges. It offers endless exercises that grow with you.

The best part is that you do not need long sessions. Daily ten-minute workouts build the strongest results.

Answers to all the puzzles are listed on the PUZZLE KEY on the final page.

Puzzle 3: Odd One Out

Which word does not belong?
Map – Atlas – Compass – Calendar

Companion note:
Ask ChatGPT to create new odd-one-out challenges or explore the companion puzzle book.

Chapter 4

Build New Brain Pathways with Small Daily Wins**

Most people think brain health is about crossword puzzles and hoping for the best. It is not. A strong brain comes from a steady rhythm of tiny challenges stacked day after day. You do not need hours. You only need a few minutes of directed activity. The secret is consistency. The brain rewires in response to what you repeat, not what you attempt once.

Your goal is simple. Keep your brain young by giving it reasons to grow. When you learn something new, solve something unfamiliar, or reach for an idea that is slightly out of your comfort zone, the brain responds with new pathways. Those pathways support memory, focus, creativity, and recall. They also keep you sharper than your peers who do not train their minds.

This Chapter will show you how to build a daily routine that works at any age. You will learn to use ChatGPT as your on-demand coach, your study partner, and your puzzle maker. You guide the tools and they do the heavy lifting. This keeps your brain active while removing the frustration of complicated technology.

Why Small Wins Matter More Than Big Efforts

Tiny daily challenges train the brain far better than occasional marathons. When people skip long periods between mental challenges, the brain loses momentum. Think of it like watering a plant. A small drink every day keeps the roots strong. A gallon of water poured on it once a month does nothing.

Small wins create:

- More confidence
- A stronger sense of control
- Faster reactions to new information
- Better recall
- A calmer, more centered mind

When your brain gets used to daily sparks of effort, everything else feels easier.

Your New 10-Minute Brain Routine

Use this structure every day. It is simple and flexible, which makes it easy to stick with.

1. Warm Up the Mind
Start with a fast puzzle or question. This wakes up the attention centers.
Try saying to ChatGPT:
"Give me a one-minute warm up challenge for today."

2. Stretch With Something New
Ask a question or learn a small concept you have never explored before.
Try:
"Teach me something I do not know yet in five sentences."

3. Practice Recall
Recall strengthens memory better than anything else.
Ask:
"Ask me three questions about what I learned yesterday."

4. Flex Your Decision Muscles
Decision making is a skill that must be trained.

Ask:
"Give me a simple scenario and let me choose between two options. Then tell me what the tradeoffs are."

5. End With a Win
Finish with something you enjoy. A word puzzle, a pattern puzzle, or a memory game.
Ask:
"Give me a short puzzle that ends today's session on a positive note."

This simple pattern becomes a habit. Habits become strength. Strength becomes protection. Protection becomes power.

What You Are Training Each Day

Each small task in this daily routine builds one or more of these cognitive skills:

Long-term memory
Remembering past events, names, ideas, and details.

Working memory
Holding information in your mind long enough to use it.

Attention to detail
Noticing what others miss.

Processing speed
Taking in information and responding faster.

Executive function
Organizing your thoughts, planning ahead, and making sound decisions.

Emotional steadiness

Mental clarity reduces worry and reactivity.

You are giving your brain the workout it needs without strain or confusion.

Why ChatGPT Makes This Easier

Traditional brain games can get boring fast. People stop doing them. ChatGPT solves that problem because it adjusts to your level, your interests, your speed, and your comfort zone.

ChatGPT can:

- Create new puzzles every day
- Explain answers you miss
- Teach you anything in simple language
- Build challenges around your hobbies
- Track your progress
- Repeat, adapt, slow down, or speed up
- Keep sessions fresh and fun

You are not learning alone. You have a coach who never gets tired and never runs out of ideas.

A Simple Script to Start Every Morning

Copy this into your notes:

"Good morning, Brain Bot. Give me my 10-minute brain routine. Start with a warm-up. Then give me something new to learn. Then test my recall. Then give me a decision exercise. Finish with a short puzzle."

That prompt alone keeps your brain sharp for years.

Your Daily Goal

Ten minutes. One small win. Then another tomorrow. You will notice yourself remembering more, thinking faster, and feeling more confident. That confidence carries into your conversations, your work, your daily life, and everything you care about.

This Chapter is not about being perfect. It is about being consistent. Consistency is what keeps the brain young.

Answers to all the puzzles are listed on the PUZZLE KEY on the final page.

Puzzle 4: Pattern Puzzle

What letter comes next?
A C F J O ?

Companion note:
Ask ChatGPT for more pattern puzzles or explore the companion puzzle book

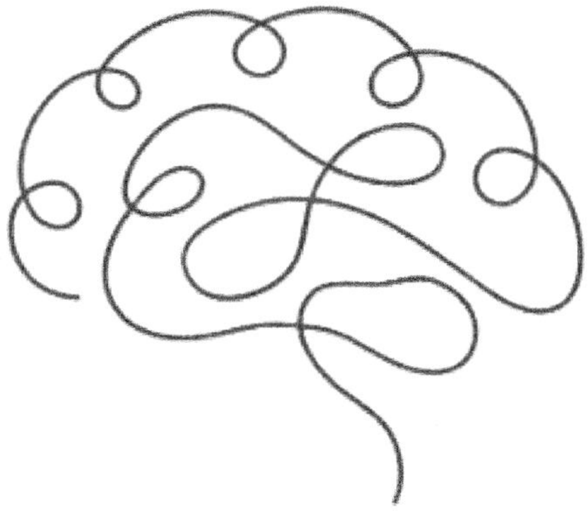

Chapter 5

Train Your Brain to Stay Calm, Clear, and Confident

A sharp mind does not come only from puzzles. A sharp mind comes from steadiness. When your brain is calm, you think better. When your mind is clear, you notice more. When you feel confident, your whole system works at a higher level.

This Chapter teaches you how to use ChatGPT to develop mental steadiness. Calm is not a personality trait. It is a trainable skill. And you do not need long meditations or complicated breathing routines. You only need short daily practices that reset your mind and teach your brain to recover faster.

You will learn how to reduce mental clutter, strengthen emotional balance, and build the kind of quiet confidence that supports every Chapter of your life.

1. Clear Out Mental Clutter with Guided Thought Sorting

Most people carry around too many open tabs in their mind. Loose thoughts, half-finished worries, future tasks, old conversations. The clutter slows thinking and steals energy.

ChatGPT can walk you through a simple three-minute clearing exercise.

Say:

"Help me sort my thoughts. Ask me what is on my mind and guide me through putting each item into one of three categories: handle today, handle later, or let go."

This gives your brain instant relief. You will feel more focused and lighter within minutes.

2. Build Emotional Steadiness with Micro-Reflections

A steady mind comes from noticing what is happening inside you before it becomes overwhelming. You can practice emotional steadiness in just one or two minutes a day.

Ask:

"Give me a short reflection exercise to help me check in with myself."

ChatGPT may ask:

- What emotion is strongest right now?
- What caused it?
- What would help me feel one percent better?

This teaches your brain to respond instead of react. Over time, it builds emotional clarity that supports focus, memory, and decision making.

3. Strengthen Confidence with Directed Wins

Confidence is not luck. It grows from seeing yourself succeed in small ways. Daily directed wins tell the brain, "I can do this." That message builds the foundation for every cognitive task ahead.

Try:

"Help me name one thing I handled well today. Then help me name one thing I can improve tomorrow."

This creates a calm confidence loop. You acknowledge your abilities without pressure or perfection.

4. Use Brief Centering Drills To Reset Your Mind

Centering drills bring your attention back to the present. You can do them anywhere. These quick resets help your mind stay stable even during busy days.

Ask:

"Give me a 30-second centering exercise."

Examples include:

• Noticing five things you see
• Naming three sounds
• Naming one physical sensation
• Taking a slow breath while focusing on your feet

These drills calm the nervous system and sharpen attention.

5. Train Cognitive Resilience Through Gentle Challenge

Resilience is the ability to stay clear even when something unexpected happens. You can train this with ChatGPT by practicing tiny "pressure moments" in low-stakes situations.

Ask:

"Give me a 60-second challenge that becomes slightly harder halfway through."

This might be a pattern puzzle that changes speed or a recall prompt that adds one more detail. Your brain learns to adapt without stress. This is the foundation of long-term mental strength.

6. Build a Calm Thinking Habit with Daily Questions

Your mind becomes what it practices. Calm thinking is built from simple daily questions that shift your focus to clarity and control.

Try:

- "What deserves my attention today?"
- "What does not need my attention anymore?"
- "What is one thing I can let go of?"
- "What is one choice that will make today easier?"

Ask ChatGPT to ask you these questions each morning. The steadiness builds on its own.

7. When Your Brain Feels Foggy, Use a Quick Reset

Everyone has foggy days. Fatigue, stress, or too much stimulation can slow your mind. Instead of pushing harder, use a quick reset.

Say:

"My mind feels foggy. Give me a five-minute reset."

ChatGPT can guide you through:

- A grounding exercise
- A short recall challenge
- A few slow breaths
- A micro-goal to regain direction

Resets help you return to clarity quickly instead of losing hours to frustration.

8. Why Calm Improves Cognitive Health

Calm thinking supports every major cognitive system:

Memory improves when you are not overwhelmed.
Attention strengthens when the mind is not scattered.
Processing speed increases when you aren't stressed.
Creativity grows when you feel safe and steady.
Decision-making becomes simpler when emotions are balanced.

A calm mind is an efficient mind. It allows your brain to work at its best without draining energy.

9. A Simple Evening Routine to End the Day Clearly

End your day with a two-minute check-in.

Ask ChatGPT:

"Help me close my day with clarity."

You will list:

One thing you did well
One thing you want to release
One small hope for tomorrow

This protects your sleep, lowers anxiety, and keeps your brain healthy.

10. Your Brain Learns Calm the Same Way It Learns Anything Else

Calm is not luck. Calm is repetition. Each day you practice even a single moment of steady thinking, you train your brain to return there naturally.

ChatGPT becomes your guide. Your coach. Your quiet voice of clarity.
Together, you build a mind that stays strong and sure no matter what the day brings.

Answers to all the puzzles are listed on the PUZZLE KEY on the final page.

Puzzle 5: Quick Logic

Sam is older than Jill. Jill is older than Mark. Who is the youngest?

Companion note:
Use ChatGPT for daily logic warm-ups or explore the companion puzzle book.

Chapter 6

What Science Shows About Keeping Your Brain Young

Your brain is built to grow. It is not a machine that wears out. It is more like a living landscape, shaping itself every time you think, move, imagine, or learn. Modern neuroscience has opened a window into the power of this growth. Doctors have watched the brain build new pathways. They have measured how quickly the mind responds to new challenges. They have seen the effect of learning on long-term brain health.

This Chapter brings all of that research together. It shows what scientists already know. It shows what people feel in their lives. And it shows why your work in this book matters.

Your Brain Never Stops Adapting

For many years, people believed the brain stopped changing in early adulthood. Today, every major research center has replaced that idea. The brain continues to grow, reorganize, and strengthen throughout life. It does this through neuroplasticity, which is the ability to form new neural pathways.

Neuroplasticity is not rare. It happens every day. Each time you try something new, your brain responds. It rewires itself. It shapes itself to help you learn.

Think of this process like learning to play a simple tune on a piano. At first, your hands move slowly. Over time, your fingers know where to go. Inside your head, something similar happens. The more you practice an idea or skill, the more solid that pathway becomes.

Your brain is always listening. It is always adapting.

A Visual Analogy

Your Brain as a Garden

Picture your brain as a garden that stretches as far as you can see. Some areas are full of new growth. Some are stable and strong. Some need more attention.

When you learn something new, it is like planting a seed.
When you repeat it, you water it.
When you challenge yourself, the roots deepen.
When you rest, the soil settles.
When you return the next day, the plant has grown.

A thriving garden does not appear all at once. It grows from small, steady choices. Your brain is the same way. Thought by thought, it builds strength.

What Doctors Can See Inside the Brain

Modern medical imaging has changed what we know. Using MRI, PET scans, and MRI patterns, scientists can watch the brain respond in real time. When you solve a puzzle or recall information, a cluster of cells lights up. When you repeat the process, the network becomes more efficient. As you continue learning, the network's structure changes.

Three major areas respond the most:

- The hippocampus, which manages memory
- The prefrontal cortex, which manages focus
- The parietal regions, which support reasoning

Studies have shown increases in gray matter after mental training. People who study a new language, play an instrument, or learn a new task show structural brain changes within a few weeks. These changes are small but meaningful. They build over time.

This book uses that research. It gives your brain tasks that activate these networks.

A Real Case Example

Two People, Two Paths**

Imagine two adults who start a similar day.

Person A follows a predictable routine.
The same tasks.
The same routes.
The same patterns of thought.
The brain stays comfortable but it does not grow.

Person B makes small changes.
Reading something new.
Solving a puzzle.

Learning a skill.
Asking the mind to stretch a little.

Doctors can measure the difference.
Over time, Person B develops stronger cognitive pathways.

This does not require perfect discipline. It just requires curiosity.
Your brain rewards curiosity.

The Power of Cognitive Reserve

Cognitive reserve is one of the most important discoveries in aging research. It refers to the brain's ability to adapt and stay strong even when age-related changes occur. People who challenge their minds build a larger reserve.

Researchers have found that people who stay mentally active:

- remember more
- process information faster
- recover quicker after stress
- show fewer symptoms when early brain changes appear

Cognitive reserve is not a guarantee. It is a buffer. It gives your mind strength, just as exercise supports a strong body.

Each exercise you do in this book builds that reserve.

How Learning Protects the Brain

Here are some simple truths backed by medical research.

1. Novelty activates the brain.
Trying something unfamiliar increases activity in learning centers.

2. Recall strengthens memory.
Remembering information is more powerful than rereading it.

3. Practice builds long-term pathways.
Repeating small tasks strengthens the network over time.

4. Variety improves flexibility.
A mix of tasks trains more parts of the brain.

5. Stress reduces growth.
Chronic stress shrinks the prefrontal cortex and weakens focus.

6. Rest supports memory.
The brain consolidates learning while you sleep.

You do not need extreme effort. You need to make a steady effort.

****A Story from the Lab**

Watching a Brain Learn**

A team of researchers once showed a group of adults a simple skill. They scanned each brain before the lesson and again after a week of practice.

Before the lesson, the brain showed scattered activity.
After a week, the same brain showed tight, efficient patterns.
After two weeks, new pathways appeared.
After three weeks, they could predict success by watching the network light up.

The participants had no idea their brains were changing.
They just knew the task felt easier.

Your brain responds the same way.
It grows behind the scenes.

Your Work in This Book Matters

Every Chapter you complete supports memory, attention, and reasoning.
Every puzzle you solve adds more strength.
Every moment of focus plants a seed in your mental garden.
Every day you give your brain a challenge, you slow the natural drift toward decline.

You are not fighting aging. You are shaping it.
You are building the patterns that keep your mind clear.
You are choosing a strong future.

Your brain can grow.
Your brain wants to grow.
And you have everything you need to help it thrive.

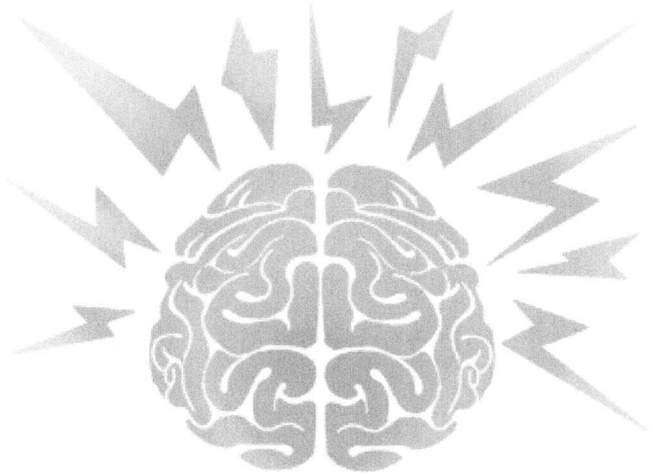

Answers to all the puzzles are listed on the PUZZLE KEY on the final page.

Puzzle 6: Word Creation

How many words can you make from the letters in:
BRAINPOWER
Minimum three letters.

Companion note:
Ask ChatGPT for more word creation challenges or explore the companion puzzle book.

Chapter 7

Strengthen Your Brain Through Real-Life Everyday Challenges

Your brain does not grow only during "training time." It grows during life. Every conversation, every decision, every moment of curiosity becomes a chance to stay young and sharp. In this Chapter, you will learn how to turn everyday tasks into brain-strengthening activities and use ChatGPT to make the process easier and more enjoyable.

Most people think cognitive decline is due to age. It does not. It comes from *disuse*. When the brain stops wrestling with new inputs, it begins to slow down. You keep your brain young by constantly nudging it to stretch, notice, learn, and choose. Daily life offers countless opportunities for this.

1. Use Micro-Challenges Throughout Your Day

Micro-challenges are tiny sparks of thinking that keep your brain awake. They take seconds, not minutes.

Try these:

• When you're waiting in line, ask ChatGPT:
"Give me a five-second mystery. Let me guess the answer."

• When you're sipping coffee:
"Give me a word. Ask me to define it in my own way."

• When you're about to run an errand:
"Give me a one-sentence riddle."

These tiny nudges keep your processing speed sharp and your attention active.

2. Turn Daily Decisions into Cognitive Training

Most decisions you make are automatic. You do them without thinking. When you slow down and explore options, your brain activates reasoning, evaluation, and memory.

Try this:

"ChatGPT, here is a small decision I'm facing today. Give me three ways to think about it."

Even mundane choices—what to cook, which route to take, what task to do first—become opportunities to strengthen executive function.

3. Turn Conversations into Mental Workouts

You may not realize it, but conversations are the most powerful cognitive exercise available. Listening, responding, recalling, predicting, and adjusting your tone all require mental energy.

Use ChatGPT to prime your brain before social interactions:

- "Give me three interesting questions to ask someone today."
- "Help me remember details about my friends so I can ask thoughtful follow-ups."

This keeps your social intelligence sharp and your memory engaged.

4. Use Curiosity as Your Brain's Daily Fuel

Curiosity builds neural pathways faster than any puzzle. When you ask a question, you stimulate the brain to connect information, form meaning, and explore patterns.

Ask:

• "Explain something I've seen all my life but never understood."
• "Tell me a surprising fact about my town."
• "Explain why something I take for granted actually works."

Curiosity keeps the brain elastic. It invites growth.

5. Turn Frustration into Brain Training

When something feels hard, annoying, or confusing, that is your brain being stretched. Most people shut down. But you are training your mind to stay young, so you use those moments.

Try this:

"ChatGPT, explain this in simple terms. And show me how to approach it calmly."

You are teaching your brain to stay steady instead of stressed. That is a major anti-aging effect on cognition.

6. Track Your Real-World Wins

One of the strongest reinforcers for brain training is noticing where you are improving. You do not need charts. You only need awareness.

Notice if you:

• follow conversations more easily
• recall details faster
• feel calmer when learning something new
• stay focused longer
• make clearer decisions

Real-world signs matter more than any score on a puzzle page.

7. Your Brain is a Living System—Keep Feeding It Inputs

Every time you engage with something new, you are giving your brain what it needs:

- novelty
- challenge
- reflection
- recall
- motivation
- tiny stretches of effort

Daily life is filled with these. ChatGPT simply helps you make the most of them.

8. A Daily Script for Real-Life Brain Training

Copy this:

"Brain Bot, help me find three small opportunities today to challenge my mind. One should be conversational, one should be curiosity-based, and one should be a decision-making challenge."

This script alone keeps your brain active all day long.

Your Chapter 7 Takeaway

The more you engage with your day, the younger your brain feels. Every challenge, no matter how small, is a chance to protect your memory, focus, reasoning, and adaptability. You are not trying to be perfect. You are trying to stay *alive* mentally. That is what keeps your brain strong.

Answers to all the puzzles are listed on the PUZZLE KEY on the final page.

Puzzle 7: Math Flash

Solve in your head:

19 + 27

54 – 18

6 × 7

63 ÷ 9

Companion note:

Use ChatGPT for rapid math drills or explore the companion puzzle book.

Chapter 8

Strengthen Your Long-Term Memory the Modern Way**

Long-term memory is one of the greatest predictors of confidence as we age. When you can recall names, places, details, steps, directions, and stories, you feel steady in the world. When recall slips, people often blame age. But the truth is different. Long-term memory improves when you use it with intention.

This Chapter will show you how to rebuild memory using small, simple sessions powered by ChatGPT. Every activity is gentle, supportive, and completely adjustable to your pace.

Memory grows through three steps:

1. **Encoding**
2. **Storage**
3. **Retrieval**

Most brain-training programs focus on storage. But the only step that truly strengthens memory is retrieval. That is what you will train here.

Why Retrieval Is the Secret

Retrieval means you pull something forward without being shown the answer. Each time you do this, the brain strengthens the path that leads to that memory. These paths grow stronger with repetition, not intensity. A few minutes a day can produce real shifts.

ChatGPT can run retrieval sessions that feel like a friendly quiz, not a test. You get practice without pressure.

Warm and Gentle Retrieval Sessions

Start with small prompts. You can say:

• "Give me three things to remember. Test me after one minute."
• "Tell me a short paragraph. Ask me to recall it in my own words."
• "Give me a sequence of five numbers or five shapes. Test me at the end of the session."

This builds confidence. Each correct recall sends a message to the brain:
We can do this. Keep going.

Use Stories to Lock In Memories

Stories are the strongest memory tool humans have. They give information shape, emotion, and meaning. ChatGPT can turn any fact into a short, emotional, memorable story.

Try:

• "Tell me a five-sentence story about a historical moment. Quiz me on the details."
• "Give me a story about a fictional character learning something. Ask me what changed."
• "Give me a tiny mystery. Let me recall the clues."

Stories move information into long-term storage quickly and naturally.

Use Categories to Improve Recall

Categorizing information is one of the most efficient ways to store memories. Your brain loves structure. ChatGPT can help you train this skill.

Ask:

• "Give me five animals. Ask me to group them by habitat."
• "Give me eight items and ask me to group them into three categories."
• "Give me a list of mixed objects. Ask me to explain how one of them does not fit."

This strengthens organization, attention, and recall all at once.

Use Repetition Without Boredom

Repetition is essential, but traditional repetition gets dull fast. ChatGPT solves that problem by making repetition fresh every time.

Try:

• "Give me five new items to memorize each day of the week."
• "Rotate the categories every day so I stay challenged."
• "Give me a memory ladder that gets harder each round."

You get variety with structure. That balance is ideal for long-term memory building.

Challenge Yourself with Real-Life Recall

Memory improves when you practice recalling real life, not only games. ChatGPT can quiz you on your own days in a supportive way.

Try:

• "Ask me five questions about what I did yesterday."
• "Ask me what I ate, who I spoke with, or what I watched this week."
• "Ask me to recall one detail from a conversation I had recently."

This makes memory personal, relevant, and easier to strengthen.

Build a Weekly Memory Plan

Here is a simple plan you can use right now:

Monday
Warm up with stories, recall key details.

Tuesday
Train with categories and grouping exercises.

Wednesday
Test short-term recall using lists and sequences.

Thursday
Work on recalling your own week and conversations.

Friday
Do creative memory challenges (mini mysteries, story reconstruction).

Saturday
Speed recall: fast quizzes, timed lists, rapid associations.

Sunday
Do a relaxed memory review with questions ChatGPT generates from your interests.

Small steps. Daily rhythm. Long-term strength.

Why This Matters

A strong memory reduces frustration, builds confidence, and keeps your mind young. Memory training also strengthens emotional steadiness. People who feel mentally sharp feel more capable and less overwhelmed.

This Chapter gives you the structure you need. The next Chapter will take you deeper into problem-solving, logic, and practical thinking skills that keep your mind engaged for life.

You have strengthened your daily routines, your flexibility, your recall, and your confidence. Now it is time to expand your brain into a more powerful tool:
your ability to reason, solve problems, and think clearly even under stress.

Chapter 9 will show you how to develop the kind of thinking that makes life easier, decisions clearer, and your brain calmer and stronger with age.

Answers to all the puzzles are listed on the PUZZLE KEY on the final page.

Puzzle 8: Spot the Error

Find the mistake in this sentence:
Their going to the store to pickup there order.

Companion note:
Ask ChatGPT for grammar spot-the-error drills or explore the companion puzzle book.

Chapter 9

Build Stronger Focus and Attention with Simple Daily Training

Clear attention is one of the strongest predictors of long-term brain health. When your attention is sharp, everything else becomes easier. Conversations. Reading. Learning new skills. Remembering names. Making decisions. Staying calm in busy moments. Focus is a foundation skill and it can be trained.

Most people believe attention fades with age. The truth is your attention fades when you stop training it. ChatGPT lets you rebuild this skill at a steady pace with simple drills that take only a few minutes a day.

Why Attention Declines

Attention weakens when:
• You do too many tasks at once
• You stop challenging the mind
• You skip mental routines
• You rarely practice deep focus
• You avoid activities that stretch your thinking

These factors create a sluggish attention span. The good news is that the brain recovers quickly when you give it structured practice.

Why ChatGPT Is the Ideal Training Partner

You need variety to stay sharp. You also need short bursts of challenge that adjust to your level. ChatGPT can do both.

It gives you:
• New drills every day

- Instant feedback
- A pace that matches your energy
- Exercises that never get boring
- Step-by-step guidance you can follow without stress

This removes frustration and keeps your mind engaged.

Daily Attention Drills You Can Use Right Away

These drills work because they require you to notice details, block out distractions, and keep your mind steady.

Use these exact prompts.

1. Spot the Error

Ask:
"Give me a short paragraph with one hidden mistake. Let me find it."

This sharpens detail recognition.

2. Pattern Detection

Ask:
"Give me a string of letters or numbers. Ask me which item does not belong."

This trains visual attention and processing speed.

3. Micro Observation

Ask:
"Describe a simple scene. Then ask me three small details about it."

This trains recall and observation at the same time.

4. One-Minute Concentration Burst

Ask:
"Give me a focus drill that lasts one minute and tells me how I did."

This builds stamina in short intervals.

5. Distractor Challenge

Ask:
"Give me a list of mixed items. Ask me to pick out all the items in one category."

This improves mental filtering and selective attention.

Use Attention Blocks During Your Day

These are small two to three minute sessions you can do anytime.

Try:
- Waiting in line
- Waiting for coffee
- Sitting at your desk
- During commercial breaks
- Before reading or writing

Short blocks of practice add up fast.

Smart Habits That Support Attention

Attention is not just a skill. It is also a lifestyle pattern. These habits help you stay mentally clear.

- Reduce multitasking
- Do one thing at a time
- Keep sessions short so you stay motivated
- Give yourself breaks
- Use routines to cue your brain that it is time to focus
- Keep a small notebook to track improvements

These habits are simple. They create long-term clarity.

For Days When Your Mind Feels Foggy

Everyone has days when the mind feels heavy. Those are the days you need training the most.

Use these prompts:

- "Give me a very simple puzzle to warm up my brain."
- "Give me one small success to help me feel sharp again."
- "Give me a tiny challenge that I can complete in seconds."

Small wins break through mental fog faster than big effort.

How to Measure Your Attention Gains

You will notice improvements when:

- You can read longer with less fatigue
- Conversations feel easier
- You drift off less often
- You finish tasks faster
- You remember where you left things
- You stay calmer during pressure

These signs confirm your training is working.

The Mindset That Keeps You Moving Forward

Focus grows through repetition. Not perfection.
Consistency gives your brain the signal to stay young and responsive.

You are not trying to become perfect. You are trying to stay sharp, steady, and confident.

Your Daily Attention Routine

Copy this:

"Brain Bot, give me a three-minute attention warm-up, then one detail puzzle, then one concentration challenge. Keep it simple and fun."

This script is enough to rebuild attention at any age.

Answers to all the puzzles are listed on the PUZZLE KEY on the final page.

Puzzle 9: Mini Riddle

What has hands but cannot clap?

Companion note:
Use ChatGPT for daily riddles or explore the companion puzzle book.

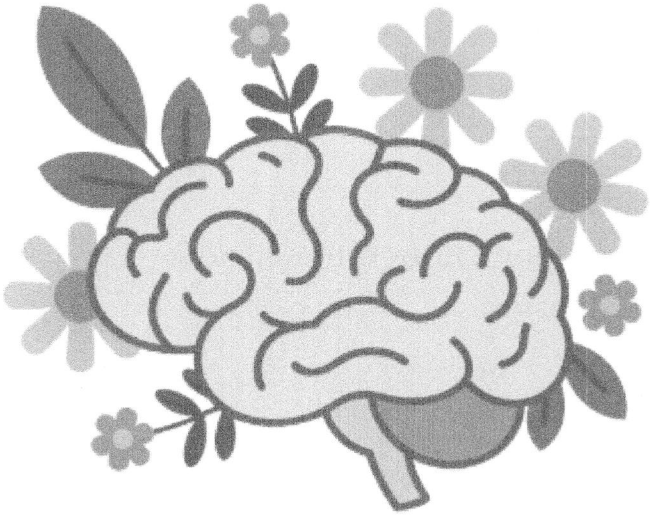

Chapter 10

Strengthen Your Short-Term Memory with Daily Micro-Drills

Short-term memory is the brain's "workbench." It is where incoming information is held, sorted, and used before being stored or released. The stronger this capacity is, the easier it becomes to follow conversations, remember instructions, keep track of tasks, and stay organized.

Short-term memory fades quickly when unused. The good news is that it can also be trained quickly. These micro-drills keep your mental workbench clear, fast, and ready.

This Chapter offers simple routines you can begin today. Each one uses ChatGPT to guide the drill, test you, and adjust the difficulty as you improve.

Why Short-Term Memory Matters More Than You Think

Most people underestimate how central short-term memory is to daily life. It affects:

- Multi-step tasks
- Following directions
- Holding a thought long enough to act on it
- Reading comprehension
- Decision making
- Conversation flow
- Planning ahead

A weak short-term memory makes life feel scattered. A strong short-term memory makes life feel manageable.

These small drills strengthen your ability to keep information active while you work with it.

---

1. Number Hold and Repeat

This is one of the fastest ways to train short-term memory. ChatGPT does all the setup.

Say:

"Give me a sequence of numbers to remember. Start with four digits. Test me. Increase difficulty as I improve."

Your goal is simple: hold the sequence in your mind, repeat it back, and move on. You do not need to be perfect. Improvement comes from the attempt, not the score.

---

2. Word Chains for Verbal Memory

Verbal short-term memory affects how well you remember names, instructions, and conversations.
This drill is light but powerful.

Say:

"Give me a list of five words to memorize. Test me in one minute. Then give me a new list."

As your skill strengthens, ask ChatGPT to increase the number of words or shift them into categories like animals, places, or objects.

---

3. Mini-Story Recall

The brain remembers stories more easily than isolated facts. Mini-stories help your short-term memory practice holding and retrieving details.

Say:

"Tell me a short three-sentence story. Then quiz me on the key details."

You will feel this strengthening your ability to remember sequences and events.

---

4. Visual Memory Snapshots

Visual memory keeps the world organized in your mind. Simple exercises sharpen your ability to hold images and patterns.

Say:

"Describe a simple visual scene. Give me ten seconds to picture it. Then ask me questions about it."

ChatGPT can describe rooms, landscapes, objects, patterns, or even imaginary scenes. Anything works.

---

5. Short-Term Memory + Focus Combo Drill

This drill trains memory and attention at the same time.
It is excellent for keeping your mind sharp.

Say:

"Give me a list of seven items. Let me read it. Then mix the list and ask me which items changed places."

This builds recall, order tracking, concentration, and comparison skills in one fast sequence.

---

6. One-Minute Detail Bursts

Short-term memory improves when you practice pulling information forward quickly.
These drills take less than a minute.

Say:

"Give me a list of details to memorize. Test me in one minute with rapid-fire questions."

You only need to do one round. The brain responds immediately.

---

7. Build Your Own Daily Short-Term Memory Circuit

Here is a routine you can repeat or ask ChatGPT to generate for you every morning.

Minute 1: Number sequence
Minute 2: Word list
Minute 3: Mini-story recall
Minute 4: Visual memory snapshot
Minute 5: Combination drill (order change or detail shift)

You can modify this anytime. ChatGPT can tailor the difficulty so it stays challenging but never frustrating.

---

8. How To Tell Your Short-Term Memory Is Improving

You will notice changes such as:

- Remembering what someone said more easily
- Less frustration when switching tasks
- Fewer mental "blanks"
- Faster recall during conversations
- A steadier, more organized mind

These small signs indicate that the circuits are strengthening.

---

9. The Most Important Part: Consistency

Short-term memory responds to frequency. Not intensity.

Five minutes a day is better than one long session once a week.

You are not trying to become perfect. You are training your mind to stay awake, responsive, and confident.

ChatGPT is your partner in this work. It adjusts to you, supports you, and removes the friction that usually causes people to quit.

Answers to all the puzzles are listed on the PUZZLE KEY on the final page.

Puzzle 10: Category Storm

List five items that belong to the category **things that can float**.

Companion note:
Ask ChatGPT for new category challenges or explore the companion puzzle book.

Chapter 11

Build Faster Processing Through Simple Speed Routines

Processing speed is the rate at which your brain takes in information, makes sense of it, and gives you a response. It affects your conversations, your confidence, and how quickly you solve problems. You can train it the same way you train any muscle. Short daily drills create real improvement.

You do not need fast reflexes or special software. You only need small bursts of focused effort. ChatGPT can guide you through every practice session.

Why Processing Speed Matters at Every Age

A quicker mind helps you:

• Respond faster in conversations
• Keep up with technology
• Solve problems before you feel stuck
• Reduce mental fatigue
• Follow instructions with ease
• Stay independent

Faster thinking creates smoother days. It reduces frustration. It gives you a sense of momentum.

Use ChatGPT as Your Speed Coach

You can ask for drills that match your comfort level. You can go slow or fast. You can repeat the same pattern every day or do something fresh.

Start with:

"ChatGPT, give me a two-minute speed drill. Keep the questions short. Increase the difficulty once I am ready."

You will notice improvement sooner than you expect.

Five Daily Speed Exercises

You can mix these into your routine. Each one takes less than two minutes.

1. **Rapid Word Match**
   Ask: "Give me ten pairs of words. I will say if they match or do not match. Go fast."
2. **Quick Math Sparks**
   Ask: "Give me ten simple math problems to solve in ten seconds each."
3. **Fast Category Listing**
   Ask: "Give me a category. I will list as many items as possible in thirty seconds."
4. **Pattern Hunt**
   Ask: "Give me a mixed list of letters or numbers. I will find the odd one out."
5. **Speed Recall**
   Ask: "Give me a short list of items to memorize. Test me after thirty seconds."

These drills wake up the brain. They sharpen the edges. They make everything feel easier.

How to Track Improvement

Do not look for perfection. Look for small signals:

- You move through daily tasks faster
- You lose less time to hesitation
- You feel more alert in the morning
- You can juggle steps in your mind with less strain
- You feel less overwhelmed
- You solve problems without shutting down

Those gains show that your brain is responding.

Build Your Personal Speed Routine

Here is a simple structure you can use every day:

Minute 1: Warm up with a quick puzzle
Minute 2: Word match
Minute 3: Category listing
Minute 4: Pattern hunt
Minute 5: Speed recall

Five minutes. Big gains. You can always ask ChatGPT to refresh the drills so it never gets boring.

Why This Works

Processing speed improves through repetition. The brain gets more efficient each time you push it a little. Short daily challenges strengthen the pathways that help you think faster and stay mentally strong.

Speed training does not overwhelm the brain. It energizes it. You will feel the difference.

Your Goal for This Chapter

Practice for a few minutes each day. You will notice your mind picking up speed. You will feel more capable and more confident.

You will build the kind of mental sharpness that supports every area of your life.

Answers to all the puzzles are listed on the PUZZLE KEY on the final page.

Puzzle 11: Short Story Recall

Read this once:
"Lucy walked into the little yellow shop on Oak Street to buy ribbons for her sister's birthday gift."

Now answer:
Who did she buy the ribbon for?

Companion note:
Use ChatGPT for more recall practice or explore the companion puzzle book.

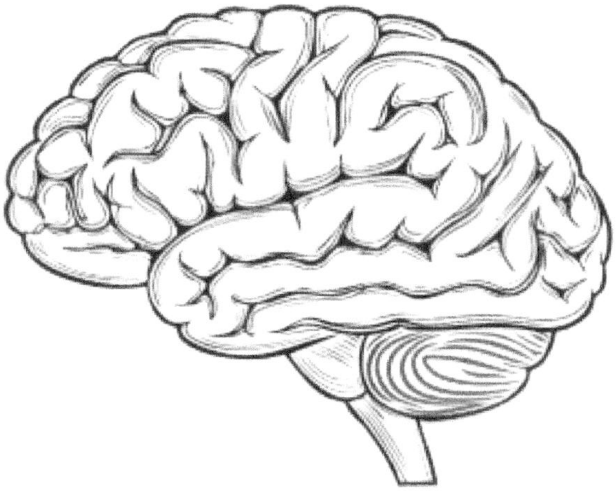

Chapter 12

Strengthen Your Executive Function with Guided Planning Sessions

Executive function is the part of your brain that helps you organize your thoughts, plan your actions, make decisions, and follow through. When it is strong, life feels smoother. When it weakens, everything feels harder than it should. The good news is that these skills can be improved at any age. With simple sessions guided by ChatGPT you can rebuild structure, regain confidence, and feel more in control of your daily life.

This chapter shows you how to use ChatGPT as a daily thinking partner to create small routines that support clarity, planning, and calm decision-making.

---

1. Why Executive Function Matters

Executive function supports your ability to:

- plan your day
- break large tasks into steps
- stay focused
- switch between tasks without losing momentum
- make choices quickly
- organize thoughts
- stay steady when facing challenges

When these skills are trained, your life becomes easier. When they are undertrained, you may feel scattered, stuck, or overwhelmed. Strengthening this system changes everything.

---

2. Build a Daily Planning Ritual

A short planning session in the morning can shape your entire day. ChatGPT keeps the process simple and focused.

Try saying:
"Help me plan my day. Ask me what must get done and help me sort it into a short list."

Together you will walk through:

- top three priorities
- optional tasks
- timing
- what can wait
- one easy step to begin with

This structure calms your mind and creates direction before the day gets complicated.

---

3. Break Big Tasks Into Small Steps

Many people avoid tasks because they look too large or unclear. That is not a lack of motivation. That is an overload of executive function.

Say:
"I need to finish this. Help me break it into simple steps I can follow."

Breaking a large task into small pieces protects your brain from overwhelm. Each step becomes a small win that strengthens planning skills and builds momentum.

---

4. Use Micro Planning Sessions to Stay on Track

Most people lose focus in the middle of the day. A fast three-minute reset helps you regain clarity.

Try:
"Help me plan the next hour. Keep it simple."
or
"Ask me what is blocking my progress and help me pick one next step."

Short resets prevent mental clutter from building and keep your day running smoothly.

---

5. Practice Decision Making With Quick Drills

Decision fatigue drains mental energy. Training small decisions makes big decisions easier.

Say:
"Give me a small decision with two options. Help me think it through."

ChatGPT walks you through:

- weighing options
- stating your reason
- reviewing possible tradeoffs
- choosing without stress

The more you practice quick decisions, the more capable and confident your brain becomes.

---

6. Strengthen Task Switching With Gentle Alternating Exercises

Task switching is a major part of executive function. You can train it in small, easy steps.

Ask:
"Give me two tiny tasks and help me switch between them with focus."

This builds flexibility and teaches your brain to shift smoothly without losing energy.

---

7. Organize Your Thoughts With Simple Frameworks

A cluttered mind feels impossible to manage. Sorting thoughts into buckets gives you clarity.

Say:
"I feel overwhelmed. Help me sort these into must do, should do, and not important."

When your thoughts are labeled and organized, your brain becomes free to act instead of spinning.

---

8. Build Mental Flexibility With Reframing Exercises

A flexible mind stays calm during change. Reframing teaches your brain to see challenges through new angles.

Ask:
"Help me see this problem from two different perspectives."
or
"Show me a simpler way to look at this issue."

Flexibility is a key part of strong executive function and reduces stress in daily life.

---

9. Use End-of-Day Summaries to Strengthen Recall and Closure

Closing out the day with a short reflection builds memory and reduces mental overload.

Ask:
"Help me review what I accomplished today."
"Ask me what to improve tomorrow."
"Help me set one morning step."

This builds a steady cycle of planning, acting, and reviewing that strengthens the entire system.

---

10. Create a Weekly Reset to Stay Organized

A ten-minute weekly reset protects your brain from stress and brings order to the week ahead.

Say:
"Help me reset for the week. Ask me what needs attention and what I can delay or delegate."

Weekly resets build long-term stability and support your planning skills.

---

11. What Executive Function Training Builds

With daily guidance from ChatGPT you strengthen:

- planning
- organization
- emotional steadiness
- adaptability
- follow-through
- decision making
- problem solving

These skills support every other area of life. When they improve, everything improves.

---

12. Your Simple Daily Executive Function Routine

Copy this into your notes:

Morning: One planning prompt
Midday: One decision or organization drill
Evening: One summary

Three minutes at a time. That is all you need. Small actions build a stronger, more capable mind.

---

13. Your Brain Can Learn This at Any Age

Executive function is not fixed. It can grow. It can strengthen. It can improve. ChatGPT guides you with simple steps that meet you where you are and help you build confidence and clarity.

Your job is only to show up for a few minutes. The rest builds over time.

Answers to all the puzzles are listed on the final page

Puzzle 12: Visual Logic (Text Version)

Circle, square, triangle, circle, square, triangle, circle, square, ___

Bonus Puzzle 12: Synonym Match

Match the words:

1. Swift
2. Proud
3. Silent
   A. Quiet

B. Fast

C. Confident

Companion note:
Ask ChatGPT for more planning or pattern puzzles or explore the companion puzzle book.

Chapter 13

Keep Your Brain Young with Curiosity-Driven Learning

A young brain is not defined by age. It is defined by curiosity. People who remain mentally flexible, open, and interested in the world stay sharper for decades longer than those who stop learning. Curiosity is the fuel that keeps the mind awake.

This Chapter shows you how to use ChatGPT as the easiest curiosity companion you will ever have. You do not need classes. You do not need textbooks. You only need the desire to learn one small thing each day. Curiosity creates energy. Energy creates growth.

1. Why Curiosity Protects the Brain

Curiosity triggers learning pathways that keep the mind active. When you ask questions, explore unfamiliar ideas, or follow a topic that fascinates you, the brain lights up. That activity strengthens connections that support memory, focus, and problem-solving.

Curiosity builds:
- mental resilience
- cognitive flexibility
- stronger recall
- deeper engagement with life
- better mood and motivation

A curious mind is harder to slow down.

2. Turn ChatGPT into Your Daily Curiosity Guide

You can explore anything. The tool follows your lead. Think of this as the easiest doorway into lifelong learning. You are not studying. You are just following what interests you.

Say:
"Teach me something interesting in five sentences that I have never thought about before."

You will get small insights that wake up your mind. These tiny sparks create long-term cognitive gains.

3. Explore Micro-Topics for Big Brain Benefits

You do not need complexity. You only need variety. Variety builds new pathways.

Ask:
"Give me a tiny topic to learn about today. Something unusual."

Micro-topics might include:
- how bees navigate
- why buildings settle
- the history of a common object
- how color affects mood
- why habits stick
- how musicians memorize

Each little topic widens your world and gives your brain fresh stimulation.

4. Follow Your Fascination, Not a Rigid Plan

Curiosity is strongest when it is natural. Let your mind wander. If something grabs your attention, go with it.

Try:
"I want to follow my curiosity today. Ask me three questions to help me pick a direction."

Your brain thrives when you explore ideas you care about. Learning becomes energizing instead of draining.

5. Build Curiosity Chains

A curiosity chain is a simple concept. You learn one thing. Then you ask a follow-up. Then another. Soon, you find yourself deep in discovery without effort.

Say:
"Give me a curiosity chain. Start with one idea. Let each question build on the last."

This creates momentum. Momentum keeps the brain young.

6. Mix Easy Learning with Slight Challenge

A young brain balances comfort and stretch. Too easy becomes boring. Too hard becomes frustrating. The middle zone is where growth happens.

Say:
"Teach me something I can understand but that stretches me a little."

This is the sweet spot of cognitive training. You feel energized, not overwhelmed.

7. Use Curiosity to Strengthen Connection and Conversation

Curiosity builds better relationships. When your mind stays engaged, you bring more presence and depth to every conversation.

You can train this skill with ChatGPT:

"Give me three interesting questions I can ask someone today."

Your brain becomes more active and relational. That keeps thinking strong across your entire life.

8. Keep a Curiosity Notebook

A simple journal builds a powerful long-term habit. Write down one thing you learned each day. The pages become a map of your growing mind.

At the end of the week ask:
"Help me review my curiosity list. What patterns do you see?"

Patterns reveal what excites you and where you can grow next.

9. Use Curiosity to Break Routines That Age the Mind

Doing the same things the same way ages the brain faster than the number on your birthday cake. Curiosity breaks that pattern.

Try:
"Show me a new way to look at something I do every day."

This helps your mind stay adaptable, playful, and alert.

10. Your Curiosity Today Protects Your Tomorrow

Curiosity keeps you mentally alive. When you learn one new thing each day, you build a brain that stays sharp, confident, and steady. You become someone who adapts, grows, and thrives.

Your brain responds to curiosity at any age. ChatGPT gives you the easiest path to start.

Small questions. Light exploration. Fresh ideas.
That is how you stay young inside.

Answers to all the puzzles are listed on the PUZZLE KEY on the final page.

Puzzle 13: Visual Logic (Text Version)

Circle, square, triangle, circle, square, triangle, circle, square, ___

Chapter 14

Strengthen Verbal Fluency with Simple Language Training

Verbal fluency is your ability to find words quickly, express ideas clearly, and keep conversations moving without strain. It affects confidence, social ease, and how sharp you feel in daily life. When verbal fluency fades, people often say they feel slow or stuck. The good news is that verbal fluency responds very well to daily practice.

ChatGPT is the perfect partner for this work. It can adjust to your pace, give you the right level of challenge, correct your mistakes gently, and keep every session fresh. This Chapter shows you how to rebuild fluency one short exercise at a time.

1. Warm Up Your Word Retrieval

Start with small prompts that activate your language centers. These exercises wake up the pathways that help you find words faster.

Try:
• "Give me a simple category. Ask me to list ten items in sixty seconds."
• "Give me a word. Ask me to name three synonyms."
• "Give me a phrase. Ask me to say it in a shorter way."

These warm-ups sharpen your ability to pull words up with less effort.

2. Grow Your Vocabulary with Small Daily Additions

A strong vocabulary gives you more tools to express yourself. You do not need long lists. You need one new word at a time.

Say:
• "Teach me one word at my level. Use it in a sentence. Ask me to

use it too."

- "Give me a word and ask me to explain it in my own terms."

Slow expansion works because the brain remembers what it uses.

3. Practice Describing Things from New Angles

Strong verbal fluency comes from flexibility. When you describe something in more than one way, you train your mind to shift quickly.

Ask:

- "Give me an everyday object. Ask me to describe it without naming it."
- "Give me a scene. Ask me to describe it using only short sentences."
- "Give me a simple topic. Ask me to explain it as if speaking to a child."

These drills improve clarity and help you adjust your communication to different situations.

4. Strengthen Conversation Skills Through Role Play

Conversation is a skill. The more you practice, the easier it becomes. ChatGPT can simulate natural dialogue so you can build skill without pressure.

Try:

- "Pretend you are a friendly neighbor. Ask me three questions. Help me respond with clear short replies."
- "Guide me through a simple conversation. Keep it relaxed."
- "Ask me follow up questions so I learn how to expand my thoughts."

Role play removes fear and builds confidence.

5. Improve Speed and Accuracy with Verbal Drills

Fast drills improve fluency in a direct way. They teach your brain to move through ideas without hesitation.

Ask:
• "Give me five rapid-fire questions about a topic. Increase the pace each round."
• "Give me a sentence. Ask me to shorten it. Then ask me to make it longer."
• "Give me a word. Ask me to create a sentence in ten seconds."

These drills keep your language circuits sharp.

6. Build Storytelling Strength Through Micro Stories

Telling a short story is one of the best ways to strengthen fluency. It uses memory, sequencing, emotion, and detail all at once.

Say:
• "Give me a topic for a three-sentence story."
• "Ask me to tell a tiny story with a beginning, middle, and end."
• "Ask me to retell the same story in a new tone."

This helps you become more confident in expressing yourself.

7. Learn to Summarize Cleanly

Summarizing sharpens clarity. It forces your brain to find key points and leave out noise.

Ask:
• "Give me a short paragraph. Ask me to summarize it in one sentence."
• "Give me a topic. Ask me to explain the main idea in fifteen

words."

- "Ask me to take a long idea and express it simply."

Summaries keep your thinking organized.

8. Use Verbal Challenges to Stay Mentally Young

Language training is a form of cognitive protection. You build resilience through expression. You build stability through clarity.

These exercises support:

- faster retrieval
- stronger memory
- better communication
- sharper thinking
- more confident social interaction

Every small drill builds your capacity.

9. Create Your Daily Verbal Fluency Routine

Here is a simple routine you can use with ChatGPT.

Minute 1: Quick warm-up.
Minutes 2 to 3: Vocabulary practice.
Minutes 4 to 5: Description drill.
Minutes 6 to 7: Conversation role play.
Minutes 8 to 9: Speed drill.
Minute 10: Micro story.

Small steps build lasting fluency.

10. Your Words Can Stay Strong at Any Age

You can regain speed, clarity, and expression. You can grow sharper. You can feel more confident speaking with others. Your brain responds when you give it structured practice.

ChatGPT gives you patience. You bring consistency. That combination keeps your words strong.

Chapter 15 will continue our path by showing how to build better problem-solving skills one short exercise at a time.

Answers to all the puzzles are listed on the PUZZLE KEY on the final page.

Puzzle 14: Sentence Remix

Rewrite this sentence in a happier tone:
"Today was difficult."

Companion note:
Ask ChatGPT for creative rewriting exercises or explore the companion puzzle book.

Chapter 15

Strengthen Your Problem-Solving Through Step-By-Step Thinking

A strong mind is not one that avoids problems. It is one that moves through them with structure, calm, and clarity. Problem-solving is a trained skill. When you learn a step-by-step method, your brain becomes faster, more confident, and far less overwhelmed.

This Chapter teaches you how to use ChatGPT as your problem-solving partner. You will learn how to break situations down, analyze what matters, explore options, and choose the next best move without stress.

1. Why Step-By-Step Thinking Matters

When the brain is tired, stressed, or overloaded, problems feel bigger than they are. A step-by-step approach:

- prevents emotional floods
- lowers mental noise
- improves judgment
- clarifies what truly matters
- reveals options you didn't notice

Clear thinking is not about being brilliant. It is about being structured.

---

2. Start With a Simple Breakdown

Most problems feel overwhelming because the brain tries to hold everything at once. ChatGPT helps you reduce the mental load.

Say:

"Help me break this problem into three simple parts. Keep it clear and short."

This gives your brain a starting point. The moment a problem is divided, your thinking becomes stronger.

---

3. Identify the Core Issue

People often react to symptoms instead of the root issue. ChatGPT can help you drill down.

Try:

"Help me find the real problem underneath this situation. Ask me three questions."

Questions reveal clarity. Clarity reduces fear. Once the core issue is named, solutions appear.

---

4. Explore Options Without Pressure

Many people shut down because they think they must solve everything perfectly the first time. You don't. You only need possibilities.

Say:

"Give me three possible ways to handle this. Explain the pros and cons of each."

Options release tension. When you see choices, your brain becomes flexible again.

---

5. Evaluate Outcomes Calmly

Your brain works better when decisions feel simple. Let ChatGPT guide you through a calm evaluation.

Ask:

"Walk me through what might happen if I choose Option A, Option B, or Option C."

This builds emotional steadiness and reduces decision fatigue.

---

6. Choose Your Next Best Step

The next step is always small. ChatGPT helps you avoid overthinking.

Say:

"Based on the options, help me choose one small next step I can take today."

Small steps preserve momentum. Momentum builds confidence.

---

7. Review and Adjust

Problem-solving is not a one-time event. It is a cycle. Your brain grows stronger every time you review your choices.

At the end of the day, ask:

"Help me review what worked today, what didn't, and what I can adjust tomorrow."

Your brain learns quickly through reflection.

---

8. Build a Daily Problem-Solving Habit

Use this short routine:

1. Describe the problem.
2. Break it into three parts.
3. Identify the core issue.
4. Generate three options.
5. Choose one small step.
6. Review your progress later.

The more you repeat this pattern, the easier life becomes.

---

9. What This Training Builds

Each problem you solve strengthens:

- judgment
- confidence
- emotional steadiness
- clarity
- perspective
- adaptability
- resilience

Your brain learns that no situation is too large to handle.

---

10. Your Brain Can Become a Better Problem-Solver at Any Age

This is not about intellect. It is about structure. When you give your brain a clear method, it rewards you with calm, confidence, and clarity.

ChatGPT makes this process simple, steady, and repeatable. You guide it. It supports you.

Small steps. Clear thinking. A mind that grows stronger every day.

Answers to all the puzzles are listed on the PUZZLE KEY on the final page.

Puzzle 15: Two Truths One Lie

Two statements are true and one is false. Identify the false one:

1. The Pacific Ocean is larger than the Atlantic.
2. The Eiffel Tower is taller than the Empire State Building.
3. Bananas grow on plants that are technically herbs.

Companion note:
Ask ChatGPT to create new truth-or-lie sets or explore the companion puzzle book.

Chapter 16

Strengthen Your Cognitive Endurance with Gentle, Guided Training

Mental endurance is the skill that lets your mind stay steady, stay focused, and stay active without drifting or shutting down. It is one of the most valuable skills you can build at any age because it supports everything else your brain does.

Endurance is not about working harder. It is about training your brain to stay with a task just a little longer than before. With ChatGPT, you can build endurance in a gentle and steady way. No pressure. No strain. Just small daily challenges that grow your capacity.

This Chapter shows you how to shape a brain that stays strong for a lifetime.

---

1. Why Cognitive Endurance Matters

Cognitive endurance supports your ability to:

• hold your attention
• follow through even when tasks take time
• stay calm during stress
• process information without rushing
• make sound decisions when tired
• learn new material with confidence

When endurance is low you may feel foggy, scattered, or tired after only a short effort. This is not aging. It is under-training. With small daily steps you can rebuild stamina at any age.

A strong brain does not panic when something takes time. It stays present. It finishes what it starts.

---

2. Start With Micro Endurance Sessions

Your brain responds best to small, steady effort. Begin with short sessions that last three to five minutes.

Say:
"Give me a small challenge that takes three minutes. Keep me focused until the end."

ChatGPT may guide you through:

- a short story with two questions
- a simple sequence puzzle
- a small logic task
- a brief creative exercise

The goal is not difficulty. The goal is duration. You are reteaching your brain how it feels to stay with something without giving up early.

---

3. Increase Time Slowly and Gently

Endurance grows when the stretch is small. When three minutes feels comfortable, move to four. When four feels steady, move to five. Your brain adapts quickly and appreciates slow growth.

Try:
"Give me a four-minute challenge that keeps my attention without overwhelming me."

You will notice that your mind wanders less. Your patience increases. You reach the end of the task more easily.

Small increases build lasting stamina.

---

4. Use Layered Tasks to Hold Attention Longer

Layered tasks require your brain to follow several steps without losing track. This builds long-range focus and strengthens executive function.

Ask:
"Give me a multi-step challenge with a few layers. Keep it simple but require persistence."

A layered task might include:

- reading a short paragraph
- answering three questions
- recalling one detail
- stating the main point in your own words

Tasks like these gently stretch cognitive endurance without pressure.

---

5. Practice "Return to Focus" Training

The goal is not to stay perfectly focused. No one does that. The goal is to return when you drift.

Say:
"Guide me through a short task and remind me to refocus if my mind wanders."

When you drift and then return, you strengthen the part of your brain responsible for attention control. Over time, your recovery becomes faster. That is real endurance.

---

6. Build Persistence with Mild Challenge

You want challenges that require effort but not frustration.

Say:
"Give me one challenge that is right at the edge of my comfort zone. Guide me until I finish."

Examples include:

- a pattern puzzle that grows more complex
- a logic chain that must be followed carefully
- a memory list that increases one item at a time

Finishing something mildly challenging builds grit. Grit builds stamina.

---

7. Train Recovery Time Between Tasks

Recovery is part of endurance. A strong brain resets quickly.

Try this drill:

- two minutes of focused effort
- one minute of slow breathing
- two more minutes of focused effort

Say:
"Help me with a two-minute focus drill and a one-minute recovery break."

Your brain learns to rest without shutting down. This reduces fatigue and improves clarity during longer tasks.

---

8. Use Daily Ten-Minute Sessions for Long-Term Strength

A ten-minute mixed session once a day builds deep endurance.

Ask:
"Give me a ten-minute session with gentle puzzles, recall, and light reasoning. Keep it balanced and steady."

ChatGPT adjusts the pacing for you. The variety keeps your mind engaged without strain.

Simple routine. Strong results.

---

9. Keep Your Brain Fresh with Variety

Endurance grows through consistency but it is maintained through variety.

Rotate among:

- word puzzles
- number tasks
- short stories
- logic problems
- vocabulary
- visual patterns described in text

Say:
"Give me a mixed endurance session with three different types of tasks."

Variety keeps mental energy bright and prevents fatigue.

---

10. Track Your Progress with Simple Questions

You will know your endurance is improving when you notice:

- tasks feel easier than before
- you can stay with something longer
- you return to focus more quickly
- you recover faster after effort
- you feel mentally awake at more times of day
- new information feels less overwhelming

These signs show your mind is becoming stronger and steadier.

---

11. Build a Custom Cognitive Endurance Routine

Here is a sample ten-minute routine:

Minute 1: Light warm-up
Minutes 2–3: Short complexity puzzle
Minute 4: Recall exercise
Minute 5: One-minute recovery
Minutes 6–7: Creative reasoning
Minutes 8–9: Sustained attention drill
Minute 10: ChatGPT stamina check-in

Copy and paste:
"Brain Bot, guide me through a ten-minute endurance session with small increases and one recovery break."

This gives you a personal endurance workout at the exact level you need.

---

12. You Can Build Endurance at Any Age

Your brain does not slow down. It adjusts to the challenges you give it. When you give it steady, manageable tasks, it becomes resilient. It becomes patient. It becomes strong.

You are not training for speed.
You are training for steadiness.
A steady brain stays young.
A steady brain stays confident.
A steady brain belongs to you.

Answers to all the puzzles are listed on the PUZZLE KEY on the final page.

Puzzle 16: Focus Drill

Count backward from 50 by fours.
50, 46, 42, …

Companion note:
Use ChatGPT for micro deduction games or explore the companion puzzle book.

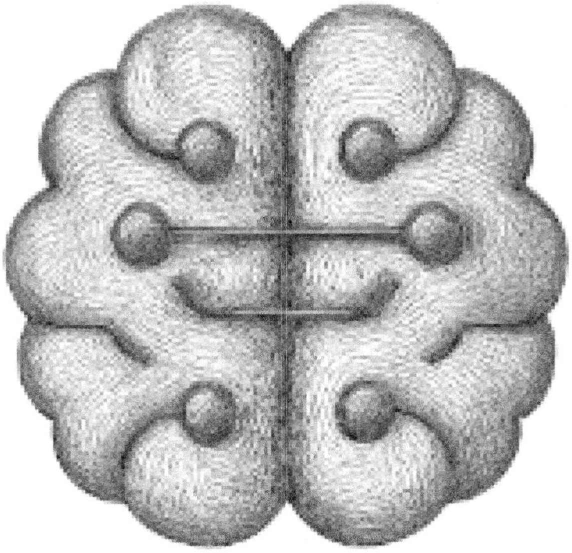

Chapter 17

Strengthen Pattern Recognition with Daily Visual and Verbal Drills

Pattern recognition is one of the most important skills your brain uses every day. You rely on it when you read faces, solve problems, remember places, or find meaning in new information. It is the skill that helps your brain connect the dots quickly.

The good news is that pattern recognition remains highly trainable at any age. You can improve it little by little with simple exercises that teach the brain to spot relationships, sequences, and clues faster. ChatGPT can guide all of these drills for you.

This training strengthens processing speed, memory, attention, language, and creative thinking. It also helps your brain stay sharp in daily life.

1. Why Pattern Recognition Matters
   When pattern recognition is strong, you can:
   • learn faster
   • solve problems with less frustration
   • see mistakes quickly
   • predict outcomes more easily
   • feel more confident in conversations and decisions
   • absorb information in bigger chunks rather than piece by piece

When this skill weakens, everything feels harder, slower, and more confusing. That is why sharpening it becomes one of the smartest things you can do for long-term brain health.

2. Start With Simple Sequences
   Your brain loves sequences. They train memory, attention, and prediction simultaneously.

Ask ChatGPT:
"Give me a simple sequence. Let me guess the next item. Then explain the pattern."

Examples include:
- numbers
- letters
- shapes
- days
- categories

The guessing wakes up your frontal lobes. The explanation strengthens understanding.

3. Spot the Odd One Out
   This is one of the fastest ways to sharpen your attention and pattern awareness.

Say:
"Give me a short list where one item does not belong. Ask me to choose which one and why."

You can request:
- words
- objects
- places
- animals
- concepts

This trains your ability to categorize and notice subtle differences.

4. Strengthening Visual Recognition
   Even without pictures, ChatGPT can build strong visual-thinking exercises.

Ask:
"Describe a simple picture using five details. Then quiz me on the details."

Or:
"Give me a pattern of shapes in words. Then change the pattern slightly and test me."

This lays the foundation for visual memory and attention, which helps you in daily life.

5. Train Relationships Between Ideas
   Patterns are not only visual. They also show up in ideas, stories, and relationships.

Try:
"Give me a short story with three recurring elements. Ask me to identify the pattern."

Or:
"Give me two ideas and ask me to find the connection between them."

This sharpens your reasoning and helps your brain build faster links.

6. Build Category Strength
   Categories are patterns. When you improve category recognition, your thinking speeds up.

Say:
"Give me a category. Ask me to list as many items as possible in one minute."

Then ask ChatGPT to:
• switch categories
• increase complexity
• add time limits

This improves speed, memory, and mental flexibility.

7. Explore Pattern Disruption
   Your brain becomes stronger when it must detect not just the pattern, but the moment the pattern breaks.

Try:
"Give me a list of items that follow a pattern except one. Ask me to find the disruption."

This improves handling of unpredictability, a key function for staying sharp.

8. Build Strength Through Explanation
   Learning becomes deeper when you explain what you see.

Say:
"Give me a pattern and ask me to explain why it works."

Or:
"Give me two patterns to compare."

Explaining strengthens clarity, memory, and understanding.

9. Ask ChatGPT for Progressive Difficulty
   As your brain becomes stronger, your challenges should grow with you.

Say:
"Make my pattern drills harder each day. Increase the complexity just a little."

ChatGPT will:

- lengthen sequences
- mix verbal and visual descriptions
- add distractions
- speed up the pace

This is how you keep growing.

10. What This Training Builds

    Pattern recognition supports:

    - reading
    - math
    - memory
    - decision making
    - conversation
    - problem solving
    - creativity
    - confidence

It protects the brain from cognitive slowing and keeps you sharp even as the world changes.

11. Your Brain Can Still Improve

    You may think pattern recognition is something fixed. It is not. You can rebuild it every day with small challenges. You will notice that conversations feel easier, details stand out faster, and thinking becomes smoother.

ChatGPT makes the process simple. You show up for a few minutes. The exercises do the rest.

Answers to all the puzzles are listed on the PUZZLE KEY on the final page.

Puzzle 17: Micro Deduction

A man buys a pet that purrs and chases mice. The pet is not a robot. What is it?

Companion note:
Ask ChatGPT for more lateral thinking puzzles or explore the companion puzzle book.

Chapter 18

Your Forever Brain Plan

You have learned something most people never learn.
Your brain can grow at any age. It responds to structure, repetition, curiosity, and challenge. It stays young when you give it reasons to stay young.

This book has shown you how to use ChatGPT as a coach who never runs out of ideas. You now know how to train memory, attention, flexibility, creativity, speed, and confidence in simple daily sessions that do not feel like work. Today, you finish the book, but this is where the real change begins.

Your brain grows through use.
Small steps. Daily signals. Gentle pressure. Steady routines.

Here is your forever plan. Keep it simple. Keep it doable.

1. Ten Minutes a Day Keeps Your Brain Young

You do not need long sessions. You need small consistency.

Your daily plan:

- One warm-up
- One memory task
- One focus drill
- One creative flex
- One speed drill
- One new fact or idea

This blend of skills is enough to build new pathways that keep you thinking clearly for years.

2. Ask More Questions

Curiosity is the strongest brain fuel.
It wakes up every system in the mind.

Say to ChatGPT:

- "Teach me something small."
- "Help me see this in a new way."
- "Explain this like I am new to the topic."

Curiosity produces the strongest cognitive growth.

3. Keep Your Brain Flexible

Flexibility protects your confidence.
You stay steady when life changes.

Use prompts that stretch your thinking:

- "Give me a viewpoint that is different than mine."
- "Give me three ways to approach this problem."
- "Challenge me with a creative twist."

Flexibility is what keeps your brain young.

4. Let ChatGPT Help You Stay Organized

Clutter drains mental energy.
A clear plan saves your brain.

Use:

- simple lists
- gentle reminders
- step by step breakdowns
- short daily resets

You do not need to do any of this alone. Let the tool carry the weight.

5. Celebrate Small Wins

You have already made progress.
You opened the book.
You showed up.
You practiced.

Small wins build belief. Belief builds momentum.
Momentum builds real change.

6. Keep Your Confidence Growing

A trained brain feels better. Everything becomes easier.
You learn faster. You recall more. You stay calm under pressure.
You trust yourself again.

Confidence grows in small steps. Every prompt you complete strengthens that foundation.

7. Build a Weekly Review Habit

A short review teaches your brain to learn from itself.

Ask:

"Help me review my week. Show me one thing I improved. Show me one thing to adjust."

Weekly reflection keeps your brain sharp and grounded.

8. Never Think You Are Too Old

You are not too old
You are not too late
You are not behind

Neuroscience shows that you can create new pathways at any age when you train them the right way.

You are building strength.
You are building protection.
You are building clarity.
You are building a brain that stays young.

9. Your Next Step

Keep using the routines.
Add new ones when ready.
Ask for help when needed.
Stay curious.

Your brain will reward you with better memory, better focus, better problem-solving, and a steadier sense of self.
ChatGPT will guide you anytime you ask.

This is not the end.
This is the beginning of the younger, sharper, more confident version of you.

Your brain can grow.
Your mind can stretch.
Your future can stay wide open.

You did the work.
You built the momentum.
Now keep going.

Answers to all the puzzles are listed on the PUZZLE KEY on the final page.

Puzzle 18: Lateral Thinking

A man pushes his car to a hotel and immediately loses money. Why?

Bonus prompt for Brain Bot

Type this into ChatGPT to make more:

"Brain Bot, give me 10 odd one out puzzles like this: three items that belong together and one that does not. Make them clear and fun for all ages. Then give me the answers and explain the connections in simple language."

About the Author

Sugar Gay Isber McMillan is a Texas artist, designer, educator and author of more than sixty books across art history, creativity, memoir and modern technology. Her work blends storytelling, research and practical guidance, showing readers how to learn new skills, stay curious and use tools like ChatGPT to enrich their daily lives.

Sugar has designed jewelry for films, television, museums and private collectors around the world. She serves as the Creative Ambassador for Fire Mountain Gems, hosts the series *Jewelry Stars with Sugar Gay Isber* on Made It Myself TV and teaches jewelry design at Austin Community College.

Her writing spans multiple series, including the Talk to Your Tools guides, the Learn While You Color collection, and memoir projects such as *Let Me Tell You About My Amazing Life,* each offering clarity, creativity and connection for readers.

Sugar holds a B.A. in Journalism, M.A.s in Humanities and Visual Arts and an advanced degree in Information Technology. She is certified in ChatGPT for Business Applications through Microsoft and also works as a technical writer for a global technology company.

Through The WOW Book Co., she continues to build a library of accessible, engaging books for learners of every age.

About the Talk to Your Tools Series

Talk to Your Tools is Sugar's growing collection of simple, friendly guides that teach readers how to use ChatGPT as a thinking partner. These books help you solve problems, stay focused, think more clearly and use modern tools to support your daily life. The series turns technology into something reassuring, practical and easy to use.

Follow Sugar

Instagram: @SugarGayIsber
Amazon Author Page: amazon.com/author/sugargayisbermcmillan
Website: TheWOWBookCo.com
For media or collaborations: GayIsber@gmail.com

PUZZLE KEY

Puzzle 1: Word Ladder

Change **COLD** to **WARM** by switching one letter at a time. Each step must form a real word.

Answer:
COLD → CORD → WORD → WORM → WARM

Puzzle 2: Memory Sequence

Read these numbers once. Then look away and write them from memory:
4 – 17 – 3 – 12 – 29 – 8 – 15

Answer:
4, 17, 3, 12, 29, 8, 15

Puzzle 3: Odd One Out

Which word does not belong?
Map – Atlas – Compass – Calendar

Answer:
Calendar
(It is about time. The others relate to navigation.)

Puzzle 4: Pattern Puzzle

What letter comes next?
A C F J O ?

Answer:
U
Pattern jumps: +2, +3, +4, +5, +6

Puzzle 5: Quick Logic

Sam is older than Jill.
Jill is older than Mark.
Who is the youngest?

Answer:
Mark

Puzzle 6: Word Creation

How many words can you make from the letters in **BRAINPOWER**?
Minimum three letters.

Sample acceptable answers:
rain, brain, bone, rope, row, brow, iron, pine, win, reap, rip, raw, war, paw, web, bar, barn, wear
(Dozens more are possible.)

Puzzle 7: Math Flash

Solve in your head:
19 + 27
54 – 18
6 × 7
63 ÷ 9

Answers:
19 + 27 = **46**
54 – 18 = **36**
6 × 7 = **42**
63 ÷ 9 = **7**

Puzzle 8: Spot the Error

Find the mistake:
Their going to the store to pickup there order.

Answer:
Correct form is:
They are going to the store to pick up their order.

Puzzle 9: Mini Riddle

What has hands but cannot clap?

Answer:
A clock

Puzzle 10: Category Storm

List five items that can float.

Sample answers:
Boat, leaf, duck, balloon, ice
(Many more acceptable.)

Puzzle 11: Short Story Recall

Read once:
"Lucy walked into the little yellow shop on Oak Street to buy ribbon for her sister's birthday gift."
Who did she buy the ribbon for?

Answer:
Her sister

Puzzle 12:

Circle, square, triangle, circle, square, triangle, circle, square, ___

Answer: Triangle

Bonus

Synonym Match

1. Swift
2. Proud
3. Silent

A. Quiet
B. Fast
C. Confident

Answer:
1 → B
2 → C
3 → A

Puzzle 13: Visual Logic (Text Version)

Circle, square, triangle, circle, square, triangle, circle, square, ___

Answer:
Triangle

Puzzle 14: Sentence Remix

Rewrite this sentence in a happier tone:
"Today was difficult."

Sample acceptable answer:
"Today had challenges, but I handled them."
or
"Today taught me something useful."

(Any positive rewrite is correct.)

Puzzle 15: Two Truths One Lie

Identify the false statement:

1. The Pacific Ocean is larger than the Atlantic.
2. The Eiffel Tower is taller than the Empire State Building.
3. Bananas grow on plants that are technically herbs.

Answer:
Statement 2 is false.
The Empire State Building is taller.

Puzzle 16: Focus Drill

Count backward from 50 by fours.
50, 46, 42, …

Answer:
50, 46, 42, 38, 34, 30, 26, 22, 18, 14, 10, 6, 2

Puzzle 17: Micro Deduction

A man buys a pet that purrs and chases mice. The pet is not a robot. What is it?

Answer:
A cat

Puzzle 18: Lateral Thinking

A man pushes his car to a hotel and immediately loses money. Why?

Answer:
He is playing **Monopoly**.

Made in the USA
Middletown, DE
04 November 2026

36545525R00071